THE CLEANSING POWER OF FORGIVENESS

ESCAPING BONDAGE AND ROOTS OF BITTERNESS

LOREATHA GUNNELS MAYBERRY

THE CLEANSING POWER OF FORGIVENESS
ESCAPING BONDAGE AND ROOTS OF BITTERNESS

Copyright © 2021 Loreatha Gunnels Mayberry.

All rights reserved. No part of this book may be used or reproduced by any means, graphic, electronic, or mechanical, including photocopying, recording, taping or by any information storage retrieval system without the written permission of the author except in the case of brief quotations embodied in critical articles and reviews.

Scripture quotations marked KJV are from the Holy Bible, King James Version (Authorized Version). First published in 1611. Quoted from the KJV Classic Reference Bible, Copyright © 1983 by The Zondervan Corporation.

iUniverse books may be ordered through booksellers or by contacting:

iUniverse
1663 Liberty Drive
Bloomington, IN 47403
www.iuniverse.com
844-349-9409

Because of the dynamic nature of the Internet, any web addresses or links contained in this book may have changed since publication and may no longer be valid. The views expressed in this work are solely those of the author and do not necessarily reflect the views of the publisher, and the publisher hereby disclaims any responsibility for them.

Any people depicted in stock imagery provided by Getty Images are models, and such images are being used for illustrative purposes only.
Certain stock imagery © Getty Images.

Scripture quotations marked NIV are taken from the Holy Bible, New International Version®. NIV®. Copyright © 1973, 1978, 1984 by International Bible Society. Used by permission of HYPERLINK Zondervan. All rights reserved. Biblica]

ISBN: 978-1-6632-2399-9 (sc)
ISBN: 978-1-6632-2417-0 (e)

Library of Congress Control Number: 2021914478

Print information available on the last page.

iUniverse rev. date: 07/20/2021

CONTENTS

Dedication ix
Preface xi
Acknowledgements xiii
Introduction xv

Chapter 1   Characteristics of Unforgiveness 1
   Definition of Unforgiveness and Forgiveness 3
   Merriam-Webster, Dictionary Definition of Unforgiveness
      and Forgiveness 4
   Unforgiveness Characteristic Questions and Answers 4

Chapter 2   The Forgiving Heart 6
   Six Ways to Find Unforgiveness and Remove It
      (by Joyce Meyer) 8
   Improving Your Life 10

Chapter 3   Forgiving and Forgiveness 12
   What is this wonderful, biblical forgiveness? 12
   How many times should forgiveness be given? 14
   The Parable of the Unforgiving Servant 15

Chapter 4   Overcoming Offenses **18**
   Practicing Forgiveness 22
   Joy Comes with Forgiveness 25
   Prayer...27

Chapter 5   Forgiving and Forgetting.. **28**
   Pain and Hurting 29
   Reliving and Reflecting 29
   Working It Out 30
   Renouncing Your Anger and Resentment 30
   Unfair Hurting..32
   Releasing the Past 32
   Forgiving Self 34
   Forgiving Our Parent(s)..37
   Resolving Resentment 39
   Developing Realistic Expectations 39
   Making Forgiveness a Lifestyle 41

Chapter 6   "A Root of Bitterness" (Hebrews 12:15) **44**
   Secret Wounds and Silent Cries..44
   Root of Bitterness Springing Up 46
   Mental Destruction 48
   Emotional Destruction...49
   Spiritual Destruction 50
   Walking in Unforgiveness...51
   Siblings and Bitter Roots 52
   The Plot Against Joseph 53
   Joseph Meets His Brothers..54

Chapter 7 Unforgiveness for A Total Stranger 56
    Recovering from Infidelity 57
    Restoration 57
    No Restoration 58
    Restoration vs. Forgiveness 59
    Husband 60
    The Husband's Appreciation of Biblical Submission 60
    Wife 61
    Forgiving 63
    A Prayer For Forgiveness (by Mark Herringshaw) 64

References 67
About The Author 69

DEDICATION

I dedicate this book, *"The Cleansing Power of Forgiveness: Escaping Bondage and Roots of Bitterness"* to my deceased parents, Matthew Herbert and Minnie Geneva Gunnels, who spent most of their lives in Conway County, Arkansas and struggled through sharecropping, racism and discrimination.

It is also dedicated to Melvin Mayberry, Sr., my wonderful husband, and best friend. He always stands by me and supports me. As I walk out the call on my life, he walks with me. His spiritual life and integrity leave me with an indelible impression. I will always love him and his compassion.

I also dedicate this book to my children: Gary Lynn Osler (Brenda) and family, Vickie Rene Young (Terry) and family, Artez Dewayne Young (Dorinda) and family, Reginald Lamonte Young (LaShawn) and family and Kimberley Felisha Brown (Dave) and family.

My deceased siblings: Marzetta Sheppard, Mattie Lee Gunnels, Sherman Edward Gunnels, Leroy Herbert Gunnels, Leola Bertha Gunnels, Lillie Mae Dorris, Mae Ella Scott and Daniel Webster Gunnels. Love Always!

My only living sibling, Onella Geneva Kindle, lives in Kansas City, Missouri. I thank God for her. We speak often, but not as often as I or she would like. When we do talk, it is such a wonderful time of conversing with each other. It is not unusual for us to talk for two to three hours at a time. I appreciate the love we share for each other. She prays for me and encourages me and supports in all my endeavors. I love my sister.

PREFACE

"The Cleansing Power of Forgiveness" is my third book. *"Beyond the Tears from Misery to Joy"* was written first, hoping to reach young and older men and women. I went back to school at age thirty-three. I received my general education diploma. I went on to obtain my undergraduate degree and twelve hours towards a master's degree. I want it to be known that you are never too old to go back to school, nor have you dropped so far behind that you cannot still build a career.

"Holy Spirit, the Deliverer, Evicting the devil and his Demons" was written next to help people understand the realm of darkness.

With this book, I pray it will give the understanding that unforgiveness can and will hide. The person will think they have forgiven their offender; however, they are only tolerating them. I want it understood that we must forgive. If we do not forgive, God will not forgive us.

In addition, to hold a grudge brings hatred and bitterness. These infirmities can bring illness and death. When we forgive, we become a free person with peace and joy.

ACKNOWLEDGEMENTS

My heartfelt thanks to Father God, the Holy Spirit, for giving me the unction to write the book *"The Cleansing Power of Forgiveness"*. He gave me the title in 2014 just after I published *"Holy Spirit, The Deliverer"*. In 2020, He visited and said it was time to write and publish this book.

I thank Melvin Mayberry, Sr. who made it possible for me to travel to my niece, Marsha's house to work on this book for two to three hours at a time. Melvin always encourages me, and I am very thankful for him.

Acknowledging my grandson, Re'Neire Henderson, for his professional, artistic skills. He was willing to develop the cover page for *the "Cleansing Power of Forgiveness"* for me. I am so grateful for the work he has put into the cover page. I may add, this is the second cover page Re'Neire has done for me (grandma). He is always willing to help me with whatever my endeavor is.

I also thank Marsha Dorris for typing and helping me with making needed corrections. She is the widow of my sister's son, Leo Herbert Dorris. He has gone to be with the Lord. I thank God for her encouraging words to write and publish this book.

I certainly am thankful to God for my five children, who support me in whatever my adventure is. My eldest, Gary Lynn (Brenda), my oldest daughter Vickie Rene (Terry), my next oldest son, Artez Dewayne (Dorinda) my youngest son, Reginald Lamonte (LaShawn) and my youngest daughter Kimberly Felisha (Dave).

INTRODUCTION

There are many facets of forgiveness. Many times, we say we have forgiven, or we say I am trying to forgive. Sometimes, we will say I cannot forgive right now, but hope I can later. This is the worse of all—"I will never forgive them."

When we say we have forgiven, many times we think we have forgiven the offence. However, really, we have not forgiven and unforgiveness hides in our hearts. With that, we tolerate the individual. In addition, when we say we are trying to forgive, we really do not understand forgiveness. When we say I cannot forgive right now, but maybe later, we want that person to suffer. In other words, we want to punish them. And when we say we will never forgive we are putting ourselves in danger of not receiving eternal life. God tells us to forgive and if we do not forgive, He will not forgive us of our transgressions.

Even though we sometimes struggle with forgiving others, if we understood God's love for us and His continually forgiving us, then we would forgive quicker with God's divine forgiveness. Divine forgiveness is the fact that God, in His mercy, chose to release you and me from the penalty for our sins. "The Lord our God is merciful and forgiving, even though we have rebelled against Him." Daniel 9:9 (KJV) Jesus says we must forgive! "Take heed to yourselves: If thy brother trespass against thee, rebuke him; and if he repents, forgive him. And if he trespasses against thee seven times in a day, and seven times in a day turn again to thee, saying I repent; thou shall forgive him." Luke 17:3-4 (KJV)

What is *forgiveness*? Assume you need to borrow money to pay your rent. You ask a friend to loan the rent payment to you. You promise to pay the friend back the next month. However, when the time comes to repay the friend, you do not have the money. In fact, for the next three and a half months, you still do not have the money. Then, unexpectantly, your friend chooses to 'forgive' the debt! This is one facet of forgiveness. "Let no debt remain outstanding, except the continuing debt to love one another." Romans 13:8 (KJV). *Forgiveness* means to dismiss a debt; therefore, when you grant forgiveness, you dismiss the debt owed to you. When you receive forgiveness, your debt is dismissed. When you grant forgiveness, you dismiss the debt from your thoughts. In other words, you do not dwell on the offence. Forgiveness is dismissing, cancelling, or setting someone free from consequences. We must forgive and set our offenders free no matter what the offense is or who caused the offense.

We forgive from the heart and not lip service. Jesus expresses the heart for forgiveness when He said, "Love your enemies, do good to those who hate you". Luke 6:27 (KJV). He also said in Matthew 5:39 (KJV) "if someone strikes you on the right cheek, turn to him the other also."

To forgive is to receive freedom when you release your offender. When we carry unforgiveness, we are in bondage and not our offender. They may not know you are bitter towards them. I always say they (offender) are on vacation on a beach having a great time and the bitter person is living in bondage. You are angry, perhaps having physical problems—maybe mental problems also. Remember, you have freedom to let go! Use these three simple words, "I forgive you."

CHAPTER ONE
CHARACTERISTICS OF UNFORGIVENESS

"See to it that no one fails to obtain the grace of God; that no 'root of bitterness' springs up and causes trouble, and by it many become defiled." Hebrews 12:15 (ESV)

Often, unforgiveness can and will hide from you. Believe me, I know because I had it to hide from me. As a young, unsaved woman, I bought a house with my youngest children's father. A few years later, we separated for good. He told me to move out of the house and he would fix it up and we would sell it and split the proceeds. I moved out of the house, and he moved into it without doing any work on it. Therefore, there was no selling of the house and no proceeds divided. As years went by, now as a saved person who loves Jesus thought I had forgiven my children's father for deceiving me. However, I had not forgiven him at all. I remember it as though it were yesterday. I was sharing with a friend what had happened between me and my children's father with the house we had bought together. As I shared, I felt anger rise in me. God spoke to me and said, "you have not forgiven him." I then told The Lord to please help me forgive my children's father, that the wounds were very deep. Once I acknowledged the unforgiveness, I was able to forgive.

We must get rid of unforgiveness because it is a life-killer in more ways than one. Proverbs 28:13 (KJV) says "Whoever conceals his transgressions will not prosper, but he who confesses and forsakes them will obtain mercy."

We should not focus on past wrongs that the offender committed towards us or to another person. Luke 6:37 (KJV) says "Judge not, and ye shall not be judged; condemn not and ye shall not be condemned; forgive, and ye shall be forgiven." Many times, we go over and over in our minds reasons why the offender does not deserve mercy. We look down on them without mercy. If it were money borrowed and it was never repaid when said to be paid back, we will ponder over what they said to get the money and when the person said they would pay it back.

Another characteristic of unforgiveness is to hate to see the person succeed in life. The person offended wants to see the offender do poorly in life. We will rejoice when the wrong doer experiences failure, difficulty or hurt because the desire is to get even with the person who hurt you. We should never be glad for anyone's downfall, even our enemy. "Rejoice not when thine enemy falleth and let not thine heart be glad when we stumbleth." Proverbs 24:17 (KJV)

We can see that God is commanding us to not carry bitterness in our hearts for those who offend us. God wants us to have a lifestyle of forgiveness. In other words, you forgive no matter what was done to you. There is no exception for getting even with the person. God says, *"Vengeance is mine"*. So, He is the one who will punish the offender for the wrong he or she did to you. "The discretion of man deferreth his anger; and it is his glory to pass over a transgression." Proverbs 19:11 (KJV)

You must not be weighed down with unresolved anger, nor should you feel no joy day after day because you are so angry with the person who offended you. We know when we have not forgiven because of the bitterness we feel in our hearts. You hate to see the person walking towards you. You want to hide so you will not have to speak to them. "The heart knoweth his own bitterness and a stranger doth not intermeddle with his joy." Proverbs 14:10 (KJV)

Definition of Unforgiveness and Forgiveness

When unforgiveness is defined, you see just how deliberate the decision is to cling to:

1) resentment you feel toward someone else, and
2) your right to get even and punish the person.

Your mindset is "you hurt me. You must pay for hurting me."

Of course, it is an ungodly, unscripted attitude! And yet painfully, it is evident in the hearts of many Christians. You can see it on their face. If you talk to them for any amount of time about the offense they are suffering from, you will hear anger in their voice. Therefore, we must uncover the dark truth behind this area of bondage. Unforgiveness depicts unwillingness to give to others what The Lord has given to you. "And be ye kind one to another, even as God for Christ's sake hath forgiven you." Ephesians 4:32 (KJV). Paul is saying "with your attitude, that you refuse to show the grace and forgiveness of Christ to anyone else."

It plants a root of bitterness in your heart. It may start with some simple resentment because of the way someone else acted towards you. Then you have a seed of animosity that begins to grow. Soon, you have deep anger, malice and bitterness which completely dominates your soul. If it is not dealt with in its early stage, this seed will damage your life for an exceedingly long time. I will venture out and say until you deal with the resentment. If you carry unforgiveness for a long time, you could have to go through deliverance.

It prevents you from becoming the person God intended you to be. An unforgiving spirit makes it impossible to accomplish what God has planned for your life. After all, how can you grow in Christ if you allow bitterness to set up in your heart?

The results of holding on to unforgiveness is very obvious; however, many believers fall into that trap. I hope this book, "The Cleansing Power of Forgiveness" will help you to not fall into that trap of unforgiveness. In addition, ask God to help you release any unforgiveness you have, and be reconciled to that person as soon as possible.

Merriam-Webster, Dictionary Definition of Unforgiveness and Forgiveness

Forgiveness – 1. To cease to feel resentment against (an offender). To pardon, forgive one's enemies. 2a. To give up resentment of or claim to requital (see requital sense 1) For forgive an insult. 2b. To grant relief from payment or forgive a debt. Intransitive verb: To grant forgiveness had to learn to forgive and forget.

Unforgiveness – 1. Unwilling or unable to forgive 2. Having or making no allowance for error or weakness an unforgiving environment where false moves can prove fatal (Jaclyn Fierman)

Unforgiveness Characteristic Questions and Answers

"But if you do not forgive others their trespasses, neither will your Father forgive your trespasses." Matthew 6:15 (ESV)

Question: What if the person does not apologize or show sorrow for their offense?

<u>Answer:</u> You must forgive because it is you who is held in bondage without forgiveness.

And Jesus said, "Father, forgive them, for they know not what they do." Luke 23:24 (ESV)

<u>Question:</u> What if I forgive those who offend me and let them off the hook, then they suffer no consequences for their behavior?

<u>Answer:</u> You will be free from bondage and God will bring vengeance upon that person. However, some of us may feel like "If I am being an enabler" he or she will continue offending people. Again, I want you to understand forgiving your offender is not about them, but it is about you.

CHAPTER TWO
THE FORGIVING HEART

"But the fruit of the Spirit is love, joy, peace, longsuffering, gentleness, goodness, faith, meekness temperance: against such there is no law." Galatians 5:22-23 (KJV). If everyone walked with the fruit of the Spirit, forgiveness would never be a problem.

Before, I address the fruit of the Spirit and unforgiveness, I am going to share a revelation God gave to me about the fruit of the Spirit in 2017 as I prayed. I was preparing my message for Sunday morning at Bethesda Worship and Deliverance Center when God gave me the revelation. I was preparing to teach on the fruit of the Spirit. He told me to look at natural birth. He said, "when a baby is born of the flesh, they are born with five senses." I began to meditate on that fact.

When a baby is born, his or her senses are hearing, seeing, feeling, smelling, and tasting. He (God) showed me that the senses are not developed at birth. However, as a baby gets older the senses begin the develop. For example, when a newborn comes home from the hospital, you can slam doors and it will not awaken the baby. When it gets to be three or four weeks old, you will have to be careful with doors slamming so that the baby's sleep will not be interrupted.

He (God) went on to tell me when a person accepts Jesus Christ as Savior and is born again, that person receives the nine gifts of the fruit of the Spirit. As with the natural baby's five senses that must be developed, it is the same for the fruit of the Spirit. For example, patience must develop so that we will not get ahead of God. We must cultivate the fruit so that all nine areas of the fruit will grow. They will not all grow at the same time.

A forgiving heart does not keep a record of the bad things the offender has done. The heart will allow the possibility that the offender can change. "And above all things, have fervent charity among yourselves: For charity shall cover the multitude of sins." I Peter 4:8 (KJV)

"What then? Notwithstanding, every way whether in pretense, or in truth, Christ is preached; and I therein do rejoice, yea, and will rejoice. For I know that this shall turn to my salvation through your prayer, and the supply of the Spirit of Jesus Christ," Philippians 1:18-19 (KJV)

You are seeking to resolve any difficulty, hurt or division and wanting the offender to be right with God and to be blessed by Him.

This is a heart that lowers the guard of the offender and paves the way for reconciliation. "And the fruit of righteousness is sown in peace of them who make peace." James 3:18 (KJV)

If you are patient, you will look for practical ways to express kind deeds and meet needs of your offender. "Love is patient." 1 Corinthians 13:4 (KJV)

You see, "A kind man benefits himself, but a cruel man brings trouble on himself". Proverbs 11:17 (KJV)

God made Solomon the wisest man of his time. If we are kind, we will take a lot and go through a lot with others before we become offended. If we become offended, we will forgive right away so bitterness will not set up in our heart.

The devil (Satan) wants us to carry hatred and bitterness. He wants our hearts dirty. If he can keep us walking with unforgiveness, he knows he can keep us in a place of control by him. If we are controlled by Satan, we will submit to much evil–not only unforgiveness but immorality, among other sin.

A heart reflecting the highest moral character—the character of Christ will forgive. Do this "with gentleness and respect, keeping a clear conscience so that those who speak maliciously against your good behavior in Christ may be ashamed of their slander." I Peter 3:15-16 (KJV)

A forgiving heart will pray that those who have been hurtful will be prosperous and be in good health. You will understand that often "hurt people hurt people." We must have a positive attitude towards our offenders. Again, considering the woundedness of the offender and responding to harshness with calmness and gentleness. No matter what is said or done, there must be a positive outlook. "Prepare your mind for action; be self-controlled." 1 Peter 1:13 (NIV) Therefore, when harsh things come your way, you prepare to control your action. If and/or when you are treated wrong or spoken to in a nasty way, you do not have to retaliate. Have self-control.

Six Ways to Find Unforgiveness and Remove It (by Joyce Meyer)

Most all of us like getting promoted, and there is nothing wrong with that. But sometimes we fail tests in certain areas that keep us from getting promoted. To help you understand the importance of forgiveness, here are six ways to detect unforgiveness in your own heart. Once exposed, you will be one step closer to your personal promotion from God.

1) **Unforgiveness always keeps score.**

In Luke 15:29 (NIV), the elder brother of the prodigal son said, "Look! All these years I've been slaving for you and never disobeyed your orders . . . Yet you never gave me even a young goat . . . But when this son your yours . . . comes home, you kill the fattened calf for him!" Unforgiveness is always looking at the score. Even Peter wanted to know how many times he had to forgive someone! But 1 Corinthians 13:5 (AMPC) says, "Love . . . takes no account of the evil done to it. It pays no attention to a suffered wrong."

Back in the early days of our marriage, when Dave ad I were fussing and fuming at each other, I would bring up stuff that happened years before and Dave would say, "Where do you keep all that stuff?" Well, I had a place, and it was all in there eating at me. And every new thing Dave did wrong would get added to this list, and it kept growing until it became a bitter giant in my heart.

2) **Unforgiveness always boasts of its own record.**

In Luke 15:29, the older brother of the prodigal son says, "These many years I have never done wrong." Judgement always says that I always do good, and others do bad. An unforgiving spirit keeps us from God's best for us.

3) **Unforgiveness always complains.**

"You never do anything for me." Ever catch yourself thinking that about someone? This attitude only sees what others aren't doing and doesn't see what they are doing. God's Word clearly shows that we're not supposed to complain. And if you're continuously using your mouth to complain about some incident of offense you won't get past it. Don't waste time by complaining.

4) **Unforgiveness has a martyr syndrome.**

"I do all the work." Workaholics are particularly susceptible to this one. Sometimes people who work all the time and don't know how to enjoy their life get jealous when other people are enjoying life. Is there someone who aggravates you when you see them having a good time? If yes, you could have unforgiveness toward them.

5) **Unforgiveness always alienates, divides, and separates.**

When the kids are acting up, we say, "my husband's kids" or maybe something like, "What are you going to do about your son?" Those are divisive statements. Maybe you have a co-worker who you stay away from as much as possible or a sibling you don't talk too much . . . why do you separate yourself from them? Maybe you need to forgive that person.

6) **Unforgiveness is always envious and jealous when angry at someone who gets blessed.**

Improving Your Life

I want to encourage you today to make a decision to start living a lifestyle of forgiveness and refuse to be offended. A forgiving lifestyle helps you become more like Christ. As you learn the importance of forgiveness and begin to practice forgiving others, your heart will heal from bitterness, and your personal growth will lead you to the promotions God has planned for you by Joyce Meyer.

If someone who has hurt you gets a blessing, it grates on you . . . at least it did for me until I learned how to forgive. Forgiveness is a decision—not a feeling.

When you pray for people who have hurt you, it is a choice. But there is healing in that for you. "Bless and do not curse them" means to speak well and not evil of them when that person is not around. And be good to them in various ways as wisdom allows.

If someone has hurt you, do not spend the next ten years of your life hurting yourself by hanging on to that offense. Most likely, that other person is not even thinking about you while you dwell on the incident for years. That only hurts one person—you.

You see, when you forgive someone, you are helping yourself.

CHAPTER THREE
FORGIVING AND FORGIVENESS

Are you a forgiving individual or do you need forgiveness? We always want forgiveness, but we do not seem to want to forgive.

Christianity is the only religion that offers complete forgiveness. The New and Old Testaments reveal to us an infinite, personal God who has a plan by which He completely forgives the sins of everyone who repents and believes in Jesus Christ.

What is this wonderful, biblical forgiveness?

There are several words used for forgiveness in the Bible: three Hebrew words in the Old Testament and four Greek words in the New Testament. The first Hebrew word is *Kafar*, from which we get the meaning "to cover", as in "to cover or blot out our sins." The second word is *Nasa*, which means "to bear" or to "take away". The third word *Salach*, which is used only with reference to God forgiving the sins of people. It means "to pardon", as in "our God [who will] freely pardon." Isaiah 55:7 (KJV)

In the New Testament, first you find the Greek word *Apoluein*, which means "to release". There also is the wonderful word *Charizomai* which comes from the word *"charis"*, or *"grace"*. *Charizomai* means "to grace you", to freely give you heaven when you deserve hell. What a truly beautiful word! The third word is *Aphesis*, from the Greek word *Aphiemi*, "to send away". Finally, there is *Paresis*, which means "to disregard". This word is used in the context that God will not see our offenses, but rather will disregard them.

"Forgiving and Forgiveness—by P.G. Matthew, M.A., Div., Th.M. The Bible gives instruction for restoring the person who has sinned. The offended party should go to the offender and show him his faults, just between the two of you. If he listens to you, all is well. However, if not you are to take one or two other people so that it will be established by the testimony of two or three witnesses. If it fails with the two or three witnesses, then you take him to the church. If the offending party repents, he is to be restored; but, if he remains unrepentant even despite the ministry of the whole church, he is to be excommunicated; that is, put out of the church and regarded as an unbeliever."

What if you are the offending party? In Matthew 5:23-24, God gives the remembrance of the offense so that you can reconcile immediately before you worship. Therefore, if you remember that you have sinned against someone, go to them immediately and be reconciled to that person. You must do that before you enter into worship.

A friend invited me and other church folk to dinner one Sunday. She served everyone with her fine china but served me with a pie pan. Needless to say, my feelings were deeply hurt. I did not say anything at that time. The next Sunday, we were in service, and my Bible opened to Matthew 5:23-24. Although I had not offended my friend, she had offended me. I went to her; she asked forgiveness and I granted it. However, I want to make it clear, she loved me with the love of the Lord, and I loved her too. She was not trying to hurt me. In fact, when I told her I was hurt, she began to weep. I believe looking back on the situation, I was very insecure. Therefore, I believe we can be the source of our own offense and hurt.

Another friend shared a situation that hurt her, but her situation would not have hurt me. She felt her offense came because of selfishness. Again, I believe I brought on the offense and hurt I felt because of insecurity. In other words, we can have other hidden roots that can bring on our own hurt. In summary, what hurts one person may not offend and/or hurt another.

How many times should forgiveness be given?

"Then came Peter to Him and said, Lord, how often shall my brother sin against me, and I forgive him? Till seven times?" Matthew 18:21 (KJV)

I believe Peter felt he was being very generous to offer seven times to forgive his brother. However, Jesus answers Peter in verse 22. He said, "I say not unto thee, until seven times; but, until seventy times seven." When you add it up, it comes to 490 times. Here is what Jesus was really saying. Every time an offense comes, you must forgive.

Jesus' answer surprised Peter. I believe Peter was still thinking in terms of justice and legality. Jesus' reply was not based on law and justice but based on the gospel of grace.

Jesus' reply contrasts with that of Lamech in Genesis 4:24. A descendant of Cain, Lamech boasted about his ability to bring revenge against his enemies. He says, "If Cain is avenged seven times, then Lamech seventy-seven times." Lamech was a believer but was boasting that he practiced unlimited revenge. However, the gospel teaches if a sinner has been saved by Christ, he now must forgive his brother without limit. That's why Jesus told Peter that even seven times was not generous enough. He needed to forgive his brother as God had forgiven him; limitlessly. "Take heed to yourselves: If thy brother trespasses against thee, rebuke him; and if he repents, forgive him." Luke 17:3 (KJV), "And if he trespasses against thee seven times in a day, and seven times in a day turn again to thee, saying I repent; thou shalt forgive him." Luke 17:4 (KJV). The disciples were surprised and said, "Increase our faith!" Luke 17:5 (KJV). This is proper. We must grow in grace and the knowledge of Jesus and increase in faith; then will we increase in forgiveness and God's mercy.

The Parable of the Unforgiving Servant

Jesus told a parable to His disciples on unlimited forgiveness. Matthew 18:23-35 (KJV).

According to P.G. Matthew, M.A., Div., Th.M., "There was a king, representing the king of heaven, to whom people owed great debts. A man who owed 10,000 talents was brought before him. The words used to describe this debt demonstrated its enormity. Ten thousand was the highest number in daily use, and the talent was the highest unit of money. Although it is not specified, we can also assume that the talents were made of gold. In his book, The Parable of Jesus (Moody Press, 1983, p.183), Dr. James M. Boice figured the debt in today's values: if there were ten thousand talents, each talent weighing seventy-five pounds, and if each pound was twelve ounces and each ounce of gold would be worth about $400, then this man's debt would be about $3.6 billion. The idea is this: that this man's debt was infinite, and he was absolutely incapable of paying it. In the same way, the debt we owe God is of infinite proportion."

This man was not able to pay such a great debt. And the king commanded that the servant, his wife, his children, and all he owned be sold to cover the debt. The man fell down before the king. "Be patient with me; he begged, and I will pay back everything." Matthew 18:26 (KJV) Of course, he could not do that. It was impossible, and the king knew it. As we studied the parable, we found that the king was moved with compassion to release the man and forgive him all his debt. Therefore, the servant who owed the large debt, was free because the king had compassion and forgave the debt.

Again, we always want to be forgiven; however, we are not quick to forgive. We are about to see the same servant who was forgiven of all his debt, not forgive another of his debt to him. In Matthew 18:28, we find this man "looking for the fellow servant who owed him 100 denarii, which would today equal about $4,000 (Boice, Parables of Jesus, p.183)." Compared to what the servant owed; this was nothing! But when he found his fellow servant, he grabbed him; choked him and demanded his money. The fellow servant of the free from debt servant also fell down and begged for patience. But the forgiven servant was not moved by mercy, nor compassion. His heart was not changed in any way by his master's merciful actions. Although the debt owed to him was not as big as what he owed the king, he was not willing to forgive the debt. He showed no mercy at all and had the man thrown into prison until he paid his debt in full.

The king heard about the wretched man's cruel behavior. Then the master called the servant in. You wicked servant; he said, I cancelled all that debt of yours because you begged me to. Shouldn't you have had mercy on your fellow servant just as I had on you? Then the master dealt with the unforgiving servant according to law instead of mercy.

"In anger, his master turned him over to the jailers to be tortured, until he should pay back all he owed." Then Jesus made an important declaration, "This is how my Heavenly Father will treat each of you unless you forgive your brother from your heart." Matthew 18:32-35 (KJV) In effect, Jesus answered Peter's question, You have received unlimited mercy from God through me; therefore, you must demonstrate unlimited mercy.

Now we see that there are two bases that can deal with sin: We see one is mercy and the other is justice. We see in Exodus 34:6-7 they are both reflected, and (The Lord) passed in front of Moses, proclaiming, The Lord, the compassionate and gracious God, slow to anger, abounding in love and faithfulness, maintaining love to thousands, and forgiving wickedness, rebellion, and sin. That is mercy! And it continues: Yet he does not leave the guilty unpunished; he punishes the children and their children for the sin of the father to the third and fourth generation. Now that's justice.

We are always going to experience offenses. However, it is how we as Christians deal with the offense. Dealing with offenses should always be God's way and not our way. Offenses are going to come!

CHAPTER FOUR
OVERCOMING OFFENSES

Carrying an offense towards others, ourselves or God is extremely dangerous. It is dangerous in many different ways. I hope to unveil some of them.

We see in Luke 17:1. Jesus shares just how dangerous it is to be a carrier of an offense. He said to His disciples, "It is impossible but that offenses will come: but woe unto him, through whom they come!"

The reality is that people are going to offend us during our lifetime. It may be our friends who offend us; a stranger has the ability to offend us; the body of Christ may offend us. Our parents may offend us; and we may even feel that God, at times, may offend us.

In Matthew 16:23, Jesus spoke of Peter, "But He turned, and said unto Peter, Get thee behind me, Satan: thou art an offense unto Me: for thou savorest not the things that be of God, but those that be of men." Here, Jesus is not calling Peter Satan as though he was Satan, but showing he was not mindful of the things of God, but the things of men. Jesus had come into the world to die for sinners. Therefore, He rebuked Peter.

Satan will use people to bring an offense against us. The offense is a stumbling block to us as Christians. Proverbs 18:19 says "A brother offended is harder to be won than a strong city: and their contentions are like the bars of a castle." In other words, when we offend someone, it will be extremely hard to lead them to salvation or give them advice. We must attempt to have peace with all men. Look at Hebrews 12:14-15. "Follow peace with all men, and holiness, without which no man shall see the Lord: Looking diligently lest any man fail of the grace of God; lest any root of bitterness springing up trouble you, and thereby any be defiled."

We need help with recognizing symptoms of being offended. Therefore, here are a few symptoms: sometimes we lash out at other people; it does not have to be the offender. That is a form of aggression. Then we have depression, anger, a critical spirit, emotional pain, sadness, withdrawal from God, failure to hold eye contact and unforgiveness is a major symptom. I believe various physical ailments are connected to offenses.

We must pray and ask God to show us where there are offenses in our lives. The Bible tells us no man knows what is in his own heart. Psalms 51:6 says "Behold, thou desirest truth in the inward parts: and I the hidden part thou shalt make me to know wisdom." Then David cried out in prayer, "Search me O God, and know my heart: try me, and know my disquieting thoughts: And see if there be any way of pain in me and lead me in the way everlasting." Psalms 139:23-24.

Overcoming offenses, we should understand where the root is coming from and that we have not yielded it to the Lord. We feel, many times, it is our right to hold on to the offense along with bitterness (root). I Peter 5:7-8 says, "Casting all your car upon Him, for He cares for you. Be sober, be vigilant; because your adversary the devil walks about like a roaring lion, seeking whom he may devour." In one sense, the devil cannot steal from us unless we allow him to do so. Therefore, we must cast down every stronghold. "For the weapons of our warfare are not carnal, but mighty through God to the pulling down of strong holds:". 2 Corinthians 10:4 (KJV). Also, what we own, give it back into the hands of Jesus.

We should purpose, by the grace of God, to forgive those who have transgressed against what we believe to be our personal "rights." I believe, unforgiveness gives Satan the legal right to attack us. "Be ye angry, and sin not: let not the sun go down upon your wrath: neither give place to the devil." Ephesians 4:26-27. When we are angry and the sun goes down on our anger, we leave the door open . . . the devil then enters our soul (mind, will and emotions) and sets up strongholds of lies. Listen to Jesus' warning. "And his master was angry and delivered him to the torturers until he should pay all that was due to him." So my heavenly Father also will do to you if each of you, from his heart, does not forgive his brother in his trespasses." Matthew 18:34-35. The evil spirits are tormentors. Jesus says in Matthew 6:14-15, "For if you forgive men their trespasses, your heavenly Father will also forgive you. But if you do not forgive men their trespasses, neither will your father forgive your trespasses." After all, Jesus forgave those who nailed Him to the cross. Luke 23:34. "Father, forgive them; for they know not what they do."

We should ask God to show what wrong attitudes we have toward the offender and ask Him to forgive us. But let us be real, the first thing comes to mind is revenge. Being Christian/non-Christian, the thought comes "get even". However, the Holy Spirit will come with conviction. The Christian, it is possible, will listen and repent. I John 1:9 says, "If we confess our sins, He is faithful and just to forgive us our sins, and to cleanse us from all unrighteousness."

I do not know about you, but I don't like to leave things hanging. I believe we need to go to the person who has offended us and ask that person for forgiveness, especially if a wrong attitude or action has been expressed towards that individual. Also, talk out the offense;

what happened and why did it happen? However, it will depend on whether the offender will be willing to discuss the offense or receive your forgiveness when you ask them to forgive you. But that is okay. You will have done your part and God is pleased.

It is wise to make sure the spirit of unforgiveness has left and is not chained to another spirit or experience. As I shared earlier, the unforgiveness I had for my children's father was hidden from me. I was in a church service and at the end of the evangelist's message she began to make an altar call. I went to the altar. When she got to me, she said "you have someone in your family you have not forgiven." I went back to my seat thinking she had missed it. The thought came what she had said was not true. However, it was true. As I spoke to a friend, I felt animosity rise as I shared some things about my children's father. God spoke and said, "that's who it is." I said to the Father, "the wounds are so deep, I need you to help me to forgive him and heal." God is so faithful, He did just that. I forgave him and was healed. The Holy Spirit, who is all truth, will validate your freedom. One indicator is the peace that you will receive. God cleansed my wounds . . . He healed my emotional wounds and bruises.

We can ask God to take away any hardness that has set up in our hearts towards anyone including yourself and God. He will give you a new heart. Ezekiel 36:26 "A new heart also will I give you, and a new spirit will I put within you: and I will take away the stony heart out of your flesh, and I will give you a heart of flesh."

Not only did God heal me but told me to pray for my children's father. Jesus taught me to pray for my offender. It feels like a task when you do it for the first time. However, each time you pray, it gets easier. You get set free. Jesus also tells us to bless our offenders. Jesus says, "But I say unto you, love your enemies, bless them that curse you, do good to them that hate you, and pray for them which despitefully use you, and persecute you." Matthew 5:44 (KJV). God, the one who gives us the grace, he will give you the power to forgive and overcome offenses. "For it is God which worketh in you both to will and to do of His good pleasure." Philippians 2:13 (KJV). God can and will cause all things to work together for our good and His glory. "And we know all things work together for good to them that love God, to them who are the called according to His purpose." Romans 8:28 (KJV).

Practicing Forgiveness

The forgiven must forgive. Oftentimes, we want people and God to forgive us, but no forgiveness for them. God was included because I know people who had not forgiven God for something that they felt He was responsible for.

I worked at the prison for women for the State of Nebraska for over 20 years. I met a young woman there who was serving time for prostitution. We will call her Mary. Mary was incredibly angry with God and said she could not forgive Him. She told me she had a baby son to die, and she blamed God. Mary, on her death bed sent for me while she was in prison. She gave her life to Christ. (She was born again according to John 3:3). She also asked me to eulogize her funeral.

Those who are forgiven, must forgive (by P.G. Matthew, M.A., M. Div., Th.M.) "Our forgiving others is the proof that we have been truly forgiven." We read about this in Luke 7:36-50. Jesus Christ was invited to dinner by a Pharisee named Simon, but He was not properly welcomed when He arrived. He was not given any water to wash His feet, nor customary welcoming kiss, nor the anointing oil usually given to an honored guest. But while He was there, a woman who had lived a wicked life came to the house. She had received mercy and forgiveness, and when she came to Jesus, she washed His feet with her tears of joy, dried them with her hair, kissed them again and again, and poured expensive perfume upon Jesus' feet. So, Jesus asked Simon: "Two men owed money to a certain money lender. One owed him five hundred denarii, and the other fifty. Neither of them had the money to pay him back, so he cancelled the debts of both. Now, which of them will love him more? And very reluctantly the correct answer came: The one who had the bigger debt cancelled." We have been forgiven an infinite debt! If we understand how great that debt was, we will overflow with love and gratitude for this merciful Lord, and we will overflow with mercy towards others.

How dare we do not live in forgiveness and in mercy! If you are a true Christian, you will adore God for showing you mercy. You will love God and you will love His people. An unforgiving person in the church of Jesus Christ proves that he or she is false in his or her claim to be a Christian. Such a person will be dealt with based on God's justice on the day of judgement. That person will be sent to hell "For the wrath of God is revealed from heaven against all ungodliness and unrighteousness of men, who hold the truth in unrighteousness;" Romans 1:18 (KJV)

We must practice forgiveness. As Christians, we should always practice a spirit of forgiveness toward all who offend us. It will not be hard to do if we value Christ's death on our behalf. As Paul told Timothy, "I thank Christ Jesus, our Lord, who has given me strength, that He considered me faithful, appointing me to service. Even though I was once a blasphemer and a persecutor and a violent man, I was shown mercy because I acted in ignorance and unbelief. The grace of our Lord was poured out on me abundantly, along with the faith and love that are in Christ Jesus. Here is a trustworthy saying that deserves full acceptance: Christ Jesus came into the world to save sinners of whom I am the worst. But for that very reason, I was shown mercy so that in me, the worst of sinners, Christ Jesus might display His unlimited patience as an example for those who would believe on Him and receive eternal life." I Timothy 1:12-16 (KJV). One who is truly saved always remembers Jesus and the cross. How Jesus said, from the cross, "Father, forgive them for they know not what they do", Luke 23:34 (KJV) as He hung on the cross. God displayed His love for all of mankind. His love is completely incomprehensible. Where and when should we practice forgiveness? We should practice forgiveness every day no matter where we are. If you have a spouse, you should practice forgiveness in your home. Parents and children should practice it. As families practice forgiveness, it will cut back on the divorce rate. In addition, children will not be destroyed. Healthy families will be the result of forgiveness in the home.

We should practice forgiveness on the job. If we forgive our employer and co-workers, we will enjoy our workplace . . . because no bitterness will set up in the heart. In workplaces sometimes there are favorites. The supervisor will overlook you to bless the favorite in the department. Please, do not keep score of the offense, but forgive. One time, my supervisor favored an individual over me. I asked to see her in her office, and we discussed the offense, and I forgave her. She got in trouble with her supervisor and was laid off without pay. When the union asked for help retaining an attorney, I was glad to help.

Practice forgiveness within the body of Christ. It does not matter if you are in a church building or outside of the building, practice forgiveness for all offenses. Paul says, "Make every effort to keep the unity of the spirit through the bond of peace." Ephesians 4:3 (KJV). We have said before and we say again, if you are the one who was offended by someone else, go to the person who offended you and settle the issue. If you are the offender, then you go to that person and ask forgiveness. The body of Christ must maintain its unity and purity.

THE CLEANSING POWER OF FORGIVENESS

We must practice forgiveness for offenses from our enemies. It amazes me to pray for my enemies seems to set me free. Jesus said, "Love your enemies and pray for those who persecute you." Matthew 5:44 (KJV). You, too, will be amazed how your heart will be changed when you pray for your enemies and do good towards them. Now, in the beginning you will not want to pray for them, but push through your praying, you will feel so good and free. There are two verses that say it all (unlimited forgiveness). "Be kind and compassionate to one another, forgiving each other, just as in Christ, God forgave you." Ephesians 4:32 (KJV). And bear with each other and forgive, whatever grievances you may have against one another. "Forgive as the Lord forgave you." Colossians 3:13 (KJV). When we practice this kind of forgiveness love will flow. It could cause individuals to come to Christ and be born again. And the church to be whole and unified.

Joy Comes with Forgiveness

While reading this, do you sense animosity and bitterness in your heart towards anyone? Be aware bitterness can and will affect your health and welfare. There are many people whose health is poor because of unforgiveness. It can bring on heart problems, high blood pressure, etc. Even suicide can be caused due to unforgiveness. At that point, I suggest you receive deliverance from a deliverance minister or one who is used to bring deliverance. They should be able to set you free. When our hearts are full of bitterness, our whole body suffers. The people around you are also affected by you because you are carrying a burden of unforgiveness. When you forgive, you become burden-free of unforgiveness. You will experience the promise given in Isaiah 58:8. "Then your light will break forth like the dawn, and your healing will quickly appear; then your righteousness will get before you, and the glory of the Lord will be your rear guard." Believe me if you forgive from your heart, you will experience that promise. If you are an unsaved person, but give your life to Christ by repenting, you too will have that experience as you receive forgiveness from God.

I have found in Mark 11:22-25 that we must forgive before we pray. If we do not forgive our prayer will not be heard. Verses 22-24 say, "And Jesus answering saith unto them, have faith in God. For verily, I say unto you this mountain, Be thou removed, and be thou cast into the sea; and shall not doubt in his heart but shall believe that those things which he saith shall come to pass; he shall have whatsoever he saith. Therefore, I say unto you, what things soever ye desire when ye pray, believe that ye receive them, and ye shall have them." What a powerful word, and I believe every bit of it.

As you read Mark 11:25, it says "And when ye stand praying, forgive, if you have ought against any; that your Father also which is in heaven may forgive you your trespasses." Some people believe a period should not have come after "them" ending verse 24. I agree. I believe a comma should have ended verse 24 and continued with verse 25.

We must understand, when we do not give others mercy, God will not give us mercy. But when we forgive, God will forgive. Isn't that awesome? God will answer your prayer. Listen to the promise of God in *Isaiah 58:9*. "Then you will call, and the Lord will answer; you will cry for help, and He will say: Here am I." Then God declares in Isaiah 58:14 (NIV) "You will find your joy in The Lord, and I will cause you to ride on the heights of the land and to feast on the inheritance of your father Jacob." There is great joy in the Lord when we live by these words of forgiveness. We must remember the mercy given to us through Jesus Christ. Therefore, we should show mercy towards others. My prayer is that you will enjoy being forgiven and you will allow others to enjoy being forgiven as well.

Have you heard anyone say, "I will forgive, but I will never forget?" I beg to differ, because one forgives it does not cause the mind to never remember it again. My intentions are to address that next. I believe once you get rid of the hurt from the offense and heal, it is not at the front of the mind all the time. If it does surface, you will not have anger nor hurt to rise in you. When you forgive your wounds will heal, and you will be filled with joy.

Encouraging Words: We see in Mark 11:25, Jesus taught that an unforgiving spirit toward someone who has wronged us, or we think has wronged us can hinder our prayers. It is better to go and be reconciled with your brother or sister in Christ and pray later than to pray to God while bitterness is brewing in your heart.

PRAYER

O God, who forgave me of all my sins which were many and grievous, let there not be found in me a sinful unforgiving spirit. How can I refuse to forgive an offense when you have forgiven me of so much? How can I hold that against someone that God has already forgiven them for? Teach me to forgive and forget, O Lord. Amen.

CHAPTER FIVE
FORGIVING AND FORGETTING

When it is said "I will forgive him or her, but I will never forget what was done to me"; it could be true. Oftentimes, the person has not forgiven the person. I contend an offense can be forgiven and forgotten in the sense the hurt, hate and bitterness has been healed. However, if hurt, hate and bitterness is still present, your memory of the offense will be negative, especially if bitterness and hatred is present. I believe you can remain hurt but will have forgiven the offense. Therefore, the memory will still be painful because hurt is still present.

These offenses can come in many ways bringing hurt, hate and bitterness. When we were children, parents and other relatives can deeply harm us. As children, showing favoritism can be very damaging. It shows up in the adults who were not favored as children. I heard my oldest brother was the favorite, but it did not affect me because I was the youngest and was said to be spoiled. All my siblings were much older than I was. The fact of the matter is everyone wants to be loved by their parents the same as their siblings.

Some children are abused verbally in different ways. Sometimes they are abandoned by both parents. Adoption is extremely popular, but when that child grows up, he/she wants to know why the parent(s) did not keep and raise them.

Dr. Ned Hallowell, author of "Dare to Forgive" shares four steps to help you forgive others.

Pain and Hurting

Dr. Hallowell says the first step to forgiveness is acknowledging what happened.

- Talk with someone you trust and open up about how hurt, sad, or angry you may feel. Let your emotions out, and do not apologize for them.
- Do not withdraw or isolate yourself. Stay connected and feel the pain, even though it hurts. With someone there to listen, the pain is more bearable.

Reliving and Reflecting

- Once you have had the chance to vent, you are ready to appeal to your rational side, Dr. Hallowell says.
- Ask yourself: What do you want this pain to turn into?
- Look for the hook. The hook is what is holding you back—It is the portion of the misdeed that is causing you to hold on to your anger and resentment.
- Empathize with the person who hurt you.
- Remember that forgiveness is not the services of condoning. It is a service to yourself—free yourself from the poison of hatred.

Working It Out

Dr. Hallowell says this step is difficult, but you need to analyze your anger and put your life back into perspective.

- Flatten the hook (what is holding you back) and rid yourself of the anger that is keeping you from forgiveness. Praying and meditating can help.
- Take inventory and give thanks for all the things you do have.
- You can imagine vengeance—just do not act on it.

Renouncing Your Anger and Resentment

Think of your future. Know that you and your loved ones will be better off once you have. Dr. Hallowell uses the word "renounce" because your resentful feeling may ever permanently go away.

- Acknowledge that your anger can come back.
- If your anger does come back, go through the process again and flatten the hook to keep moving forward.

I had a friend who shared that her mother gave her and her sister to the grandmother. The grandmother was her mother's mother. The grandmother stayed close to my friend's mother. My friend's mother was remarried and had additional children. My friend and her sister suffered deep hurt, hatred and bitterness. They were both obese with severe health issues. My friend passed away. She seemed to have never received answers to her questions. She told me more than once, "I don't know why she did not raise me and my sister. She raised the other children."

My friend passed at an incredibly early age; she was a Christian who loved the Lord. I believe she forgave her mother, but still suffered from the wounds of hurt. Many times, as she would talk about her mother not raising her, she would cry aloud. I would feel helpless not knowing what to do.

If you live long enough, chances are you will be hurt by someone you counted on to be your best friend. If you are like me, you do not allow your hurt to fester. When hurt festers, it affects our joy. When that happens, you have entered the first stage of forgiveness. What will hurt me may not hurt you.

To illustrate how something that may look insignificant to an outsider, I would like to share a story about a hurt I felt once. It is important to start by saying my sibling I am next to is almost nine years older than I am. When I have made friends, to me they are like a sister or a brother. The friend I spoke about earlier was a good friend who was a true friend.

The hurt that I am about to share was with an associate. We were not close friends, but I was seeking another close friend. Of course, close friendship comes when both people are engaged to have it. I realized later it was not possible to be best friends. However, we became friends. The hurt came when I would reach out to the person for prayer and their help did not seem like they cared. Perhaps she did care but did not show it. Everyone is not cut out to be best friends. Maybe I should say sometimes they have been hurt by someone and it causes them to draw back on relationships. However, when you give your all and it is not reciprocated, it hurts. Whatever I did, I did unto God never expecting to be repaid.

"Whatever you do, work at it with all your heart, as working for the Lord, not for human masters". Colossians 3:23 (NIV) Remember, I said I do not allow offense to fester. I called for a meeting to solve the hurt I had experienced. That way, hurt nor bitterness could have a chance to set up in my heart.

Unfair Hurting

I call unfair hurt when a person has no intentions to hurt you. My brother seemed to be upset because his wife passed away. He stood by her coffin and said, "you went off and left me." I read a story where the husband hung himself and left a wife and children behind. I wonder if he felt like he had to end his life. Was he to blame for the deep pain he left behind? Should his wife forgive him? To me, it was a selfish move, but I believe she must forgive him. In addition, one must wrong you for you to owe forgiveness to them. I used the word owe because God says we must forgive.

Releasing the Past

To forgive, we must release the past. When we decided to forgive our offender, we are also releasing the past. You are being released from bondage. After all, you are the one being held captive. Your offender may or may not realize what hurt they have brought to you. Therefore he/she may be in Cancun on the beach having the time of their life. Maybe you stopped calling or speaking to the person, but never shared the offense you felt from them when it happened.

Forgiveness is such an important subject that I feel compelled to keep explaining its significance. When we hold unforgiveness inside, we are holding on to anger, hatred, bitterness and sometimes resentment. These emotions continually keep us reliving what happened to us. Over time, the emotions can be pushed to the subconscious, but they are still there. You will know, because if you think about it and you will, anger will rise from inside of you. You will be just as upset as you were the day it happened to you.

It does not matter what the offense or issue was whether minute or life-shatteringly traumatic, you must forgive and move on, letting it go. To forgive someone does not mean that you condone what they did to you. But when you release them by forgiving them, you also release yourself. As long as you hold on to unforgiveness, you are thinking about how wrong you were treated. Also, the enemy may or will begin to encourage you into getting even with the person who offended you. But I ask you to remember what the Lord says in Romans 12:17-19. "Recompense to no man evil for evil. Provide things honest in the sight of all men. If it be possible, as much as lieth within you, live peaceably with all men. Dearly beloved, avenge not yourselves, but rather give place unto wrath: for it is written, Vengeance is mine; I will repay, saith the Lord."

Some people hold on to their anger for years. They refuse to forgive or let go. I might add, sometimes the person will die without forgiving the person who hurt them, and vice versa. The person who died without forgiving it is not a good thing. I have shared with you that God said if we do not forgive, He will not forgive us. The person who is still living has a chance to forgive the person who died. And they cannot move on with life without forgiving and letting go even though the person is dead. They will be living a life directed by their anger and hurt.

If we choose to get rid of the bad and move forward with the good, we can keep a sense of direction. But if we focus on the bad things that happened in our lives, we will continually be in our own dark place or dark thoughts. That will divert us from what we really want in life.

If you feel like your life is going nowhere, I suggest you should look back to see if there is any unforgiveness in your past. Remember, we must forgive any and everyone, including yourself. So many people go through life burdened with guilt for past mistakes. Forgive yourself and get rid of the burden and let it go. Next, we will look at forgiving self and know how to deal with it.

<u>Forgiving Self</u>

Listen, life is in the now. The past is the past. It is finished and cannot be changed. There is nothing you can do now to change the past. Yet it is amazing how many people today are consumed with anger or guilt about their past. I know I am one of those people who has walked there. I want to say to you if you are one of those people, you have power, the power to make your own choices, to act over your life and make a difference in the now. However, you have no power over the past and no guarantee of power in the future.

If you want to be free and released from the past, you must forgive yourself. I reiterate, forgive everyone, especially yourself. I know how hard and how difficult it is to overcome our human feelings of anger, guilt, resentment, and fear. I will share my story later. We may feel justified to not forgive, even ourselves and the right to have those emotions and experience them. However, these emotions can be very damaging. You should accept the emotions but let them go. Until you do, you will be a victim to your own emotions.

I am going to ask you to look around yourself. Have you noticed anyone like that? They have some tragic thing that happened in their life, and they blame themselves and they are truly angry. No matter how justified their emotions are, it is no good to them because the past cannot be changed. It is not the events of our life, but how we respond to them that define the bliss and success of our lives.

I want to share some excerpts from Robert D. Jones' book: *"I Just Can't Forgive Myself"*. Sally and Carl's marriage of thirteen months was shaky at best. One day, Sally discovered she was pregnant. Not wanting to interrupt her new law career and greatly fearing motherhood, she secretly got an abortion. When Carl found out a year later, he exploded and walked out. They eventually got a divorce. Robert D. Jones went on to say that Sally got saved five years later. Of course, as the story went on, the enemy brought condemnation on her. She began to suffer from guilt. We can study the Bible from front to back and will not find where it teaches us to forgive self. You will not find self-forgiveness either by example or precept. The Bible teaches that God will forgive us when we forgive others and that we must forgive each other. However, it teaches nothing on internal forgiveness (self-forgiveness). Anyone who is struggling with recrimination has a real problem and needs help.

Perhaps Sally needed to understand and receive God's forgiveness. This would help her or anyone to rise above "I just can't forgive myself". In addition, maybe the person has not gripped the entirety and depth of God's forgiving grace and power. "Know ye not that the unrighteous shall not inherit the kingdom of God? Be not deceived: neither fornicators, nor idolators, nor adulterers, nor effeminate, nor abusers of themselves with mankind, Nor thieves, nor covetous, nor drunkards, nor revilers, nor extortioners, shall inherit the kingdom of God. And such were some of you: but ye are washed, but ye are sanctified, but ye are justified in the name of the Lord Jesus, and by the Spirit of our God." I Corinthians 6:9-11 (KJV). He/she disbelieves the truth that God can and will forgive sin no matter how big it is. We are the ones who see sin in different sizes, God does not.

When we say, "I just cannot forgive myself", maybe we are really saying, "I cannot believe I did that". That is the way I felt when I could not forgive myself. It was 2007 (July) when a team came to Omaha to help transform Omaha. They came from Fiji and as a group we would enter people's homes. Those homes that the owners had signed up for ministry. I got some of my children to sign up for ministry. I wanted all my children to sign up. I went to one of them and had a talk with them before the team went out to their home. I said, now when they come be very open with them. Tell them how things were when you were a young child. I was told, "mom, I am okay—that's you." I was still carrying guilt. However, when that was said to me it felt like a burden was lifted off of me. I was a single mom. I was a hard-working woman. On one hand, I was a good mother and on the other hand, I could have been a better mother. Remember no one is perfect. We make mistakes on this journey. At 42 years old, I returned to Christ. I had gotten saved at age 8 or 9 years of age. I had strayed from the Lord as an adult. When I rededicated my life to God shame and guilt plagued me. I would think about the things I did not do and how I could have done better. It was never about the good things that I had done for my children. 2007 God set me completely free from "I just cannot forgive myself." I forgave myself and God also forgave me. I pray the cleansing power of forgiveness will help many people.

So many are living in bondage of unforgiveness causing in-depth health issues:

- Cancer
- High Blood Pressure
- Mental Issues (Destroying Relationships)
- Heart Problems

These health issues come through hatred, a root of bitterness and fear. Hebrews 12:15. "See to it that no one falls short of the grace of God and that no bitter root grows up to cause trouble and defile many."

So, forgive others, receive forgiveness, and forgive yourself.

As I think on the effects of unforgiveness, the need to be forgiven and self-forgiveness, I believe it is somewhat different for self-forgiveness. With self-forgiveness, of course, guilt and shame plagues you, but depression can also develop. With depression, it is possible you will contemplate suicide. Therefore, again I urge all forgiveness but especially self-forgiveness.

Forgiving Our Parent(s)

I don't remember holding a grudge or unforgiveness for my parents. I had a decent childhood. I suffered no abuse. I always had food and never went hungry. I also had decent clothes to wear. It may not have been what I wanted to eat or wear all the time. When I grew up, you ate and wore whatever your parents gave you and you said nothing. Unlike this era, the children tell their parents what they want to eat and wear.

I noticed during this era that some children grow up with total disrespect for their parents. It seems to happen a lot in families with wealth. It is thought the child/children are given everything. That when Christmas comes, they don't appreciate gifts because they already have every toy and game you can name. Sometimes they grow up and kill the parents. When asked why, the excuse is, enough was never done for them.

Here is a different story. The Menendez twins had a different excuse for allegedly killing both parents. It happened in 1989. According to Jordon Zakarin, who at the time was a New York-based writer and editor, that August 20, 1989, Jose' and Mary "Kitty" Menendez were shot to death in their Beverly Hills home. Lyle and Erik Menendez were found guilty in 1990 for the murder of their parents. They were sentenced to life in prison. In the article it stated, Jose was a Cuban immigrant who worked his way to the top in society. The brothers were 18 and 19 years of age at the time of killing their parents. Erik said they did it to put their mother out of her misery. They claimed the father was abusive according to the article. Also, the brothers claimed that their father's reign of terror went beyond emotional abuse and the pressure of high expectations. Jose', they said, had molested them since childhood. They made a claim that was filled with graphic descriptions that shocked the nation and split friends and family members. A cousin told ABC News that she believed Lyle because he had told her similar things when he was a child.

If what the Menendez twins claim is true, you would think they were filled with hatred, bitterness, and fear. Of course, murder was not the answer. With the alleged murders, many lives were affected and destroyed. Believe me, there are some still holding a grudge against the parents because of what they believe they learned about Jose' and Mary "Kitty" Menendez. And some still hold a grudge against the brothers, Lyle and Erik Menendez, for taking the lives of their parents. My prayer is they will let go and forgive. In addition, the Menendez twins will forgive themselves giving their lives to Jesus. Without accepting Jesus as Lord, they may not believe God can or will forgive them of murder. And if what they said about their parents is true, they will forgive them and let go of the hurt that was done to them.

The former swim team coach told the Los Angeles Times in 1990, "But he was completely overbearing it had the opposite effect. Erik had so much less confidence because nothing he ever did was ever good enough. Therefore, their (the twins) evil emotions took over their tribal family consciousness. Which makes it worse because it demands justice if you believe you have been wronged. I believe they were susceptible to illness and depression which led to the murder of their parents.

Forgiving our parents sometimes is not easy. It depends on what the offense is that occurred between the parent and offspring. "Forgiving our parents is a core task of adulthood, and one of the most crucial kinds of forgiveness. We see our parents in our mates, in our friends, in our bosses, even in our children. When we have felt rejected by a parent and have remained in that state, we will inevitably feel rejected by these important others as well."

Letting our parents off the hook, Psychologist Robert Karen says, "is the first step towards happiness, self-acceptance and maturity. Here are some thoughts to help the healing begin:

Resolving Resentment

Nursing resentment toward a parent does more than keep that parent in the doghouse. We get stuck there too, forever the child, the victim, the have-not in the realm of love. Strange as it may seem, a grudge is a kind of clinging, a way of not separating, and when we hold a grudge against a parent, we are clinging not just to the parent, but more specifically to the bad part of the parent. It is as if we don't want to live our lives until we have this resolved and feel the security of their unconditional love. We do so for good reasons psychologically. But the result is just the opposite: We stay locked into the badness, and we do not grow up.

Developing Realistic Expectations

"The sins of parents are among the most difficult to forgive. We expect the world of them, and we do not wish to lower our expectations. Decade after decade, we hold out the hope, often unconsciously, that they will finally do right by us. We want them to own up to all their misdeeds, to apologize, to make heartfelt pleas for our forgiveness. We want our parent to embrace us, to tell us they know we were good children, to undo the favoritism they've shown to a brother or sister, to take back their hurtful criticisms, to give us praise."

This information by Robert Karen made me remember a hurt delivered by my mother. I said earlier I had no grudge against my parents. I really do not have a grudge, but I felt hurt surface. It is not a deep hurt, but I remember my mother comparing me to my female friends. She said to me one day, "why can't you be more like those Smith girls?" I am not sure why she made the comparison. But I have never forgotten her remarks and I made sure I never compared my children. If I see my children making a slight difference with their children, I say to them, "make sure you do not compare your children because each one of them are different." Of course, I have long ago forgiven my mother. She did not know that her statement hurt me. Hold on to the good and let go of the bad.

No doubt most parents love their children with a few exceptions. No parent is perfect; therefore, I believe everyone has childhood wounds. The wound may be shallow like the one I just shared with you. My prayer is that the good will outweigh the hurtful things. Therefore, your love will remain strong for your parents. As they grow older and need your help, you will be there for them.

I understand every household is not the same. Some parents are selfish and mean. They hand out rejection and brutality as though they are great gifts. Many of their misdeeds and character flaws come down through their bloodlines. Their parents were abused as children. As you raise your children, hold on to the good things and get rid of the bad. Our parents are our role models. However, we must not use everything we heard or saw. For example, when something got broken in our house and my mother asked who did it. If no one confessed to it, she whipped everyone. When I started a family, I am ashamed to say I did the very same thing.

If you are angry at your mother or dad, forgive them and allow them back into your heart. Try to understand the limitations they labored under and feel compassion for them. Our compassion should push our pain aside and we should have compassion for the pain we caused them as we grew up and as adults.

Making Forgiveness a Lifestyle

Every day you rise from your night's sleep, be ready to forgive any and all offenses. Getting to a place of forgiveness, some say "it is complicated. We must be ready to forgive. The deeper the wound, the harder it is to forgive our parents." I beg the difference. If we love as God has taught us to love, it is not a hard task, especially when we look at what He did for each of us. He sent His son to die for all of mankind that we can have our sins forgiven and have eternal life. Therefore, we should be willing to forgive all people who offend us or have offended us.

God will give you the strength along with love to forgive. Holding a grudge is one of the most burdensome things you can do. But when you let go of the grudge and forgive, it is worth having for many different reasons.

I am sharing a lot on forgiving parents because, in my opinion, it can be the most devastating thing for the family. Of course, any grudge and unforgiveness destroys relationships. We know that it can destroy relationships with siblings, friends, church members and leaders. Unforgiveness can also cause grudges to develop against politicians. A young lady had unforgiveness for former President Obama and confessed it in a prayer meeting.

I want to share a mother/son relationship and how I saw it develop over the years. The mother was a young mother. She gave birth to her son right after she graduated from high school. Employment was not good in the small town she lived in. The mother moved out the state leaving her son with her mother. The mother said, "I am leaving Johnny here with mama so I can work and not worry about him getting hit by a car." I remember her saying that as if it were yesterday. However, it was one of the worse mistakes she could make. He grew up to be thirteen years old and decided to leave his grandmother and live with his father out of state. Later years, Johnny's mother moved to the same town he was living in. Johnny was moved out and living on his own. His mother wanted him to live with her, but Johnny had met the love of his life. With his getting married, the conflicts started.

The relationship was damaged from the start because she did not raise him. I am almost sure that he felt rejected and abandoned by her. They were both hurt by the situation and went through a lot because he was left with his grandmother. I knew they (mother and son) loved each other and forgave each other for their misgivings. I had the opportunity to pray with Johnny and he forgave his mother. Praise God. He did not get to tell her he forgave her because she was deceased. She was a God-fearing person and I believe she forgave him for whatever wrong she felt she received from him.

I decided to close this chapter with another single mother and children situation. I urge you to keep in mind as I share, all parents make mistakes raising their children because no one is perfect.

2018, God revealed another situation in my life that was hidden to me. However, I had met with my children after giving my life to Christ and asked each child for forgiveness. Each child said, "mama, I forgive you." I received my forgiveness. However, I never named off things when asking for forgiveness. So, the enemy tried to bring up some old hurts but God revealed and brought healing. The hurt was from many years ago. I had no problem with asking for forgiveness again and was granted it. I thank God we have no unforgiveness in our hearts. Matthew 6:15 says we must forgive because if we do not forgive, God will not forgive us. We are all saved. I believe saved people who understand God's word will forgive their offender. No matter what the offense is or how harsh it is, Love covers all things. Praise God!!!

CHAPTER SIX
"A ROOT OF BITTERNESS" (HEBREWS 12:15)

<u>Secret Wounds and Silent Cries</u>

When I think about secret wounds and silent cries, I wonder how many young boys and girls are subject to being hurt and no one knows. Or a wife who is being controlled and abused by her husband. Then biological fathers are tipping in and molesting their daughters and/or sons. I am so sorry to say priests violate the young boys who are in training as altar boys. Joyce Meyers is incredibly open about the abuse of her father. She has shared how he had sex with her. And tried to exchange her body for a traffic ticket he owed with a police officer. Joyce forgave her father and took care of him until his death.

In Dewey Bertolini's book, *"Secret Wounds and Silent Cries"*, he shares much regarding bitterness. He says, "Bitterness—It's more than Skin Deep." He further states "Root: not a glamorous word by anybody's standard, but used in this context, 'root' serves as a helpful metaphor. "Every spring, with spade in hand, my son and I step out onto the lawn, ready to reclaim the precious turf we have lost to the weeds. We always remind each other, "whenever you pull out a weed, be sure you take it up by its roots."

THE CLEANSING POWER OF FORGIVENESS

I agree with Dewey Bertolini that the word root serves as a metaphor when talking about bitterness. I am going to use a weed that most of us can agree has an amazing root. It seems that you cannot kill or get rid of it unless you dig up the root. That weed is a dandelion weed. As I looked for the correct spelling for dandelion, I found you can eat them. The green leaves and yellow flower can be eaten in a salad. Also, the leaves can be cooked in turnip greens or spinach. The roots can be used to substitute coffee after dried out. In addition, served as an excellent source of Vitamins A, C and K, they also contain Vitamin E, folate, and small amounts of B Vitamin. Even though it is said dandelion greens provide a substantial taste and can be eaten, they create a lot of heartache spring and summer. Oftentimes, yards are full of them. Homeowners are spraying with solutions to kill them but save the grass. My advice is to catch them before the yard is covered and dig them up by the root. Otherwise, it is exceedingly difficult to get rid of them. That is the way it is with bitterness that is in the heart of man due to unforgiveness. You must deal with the root of unforgiveness to destroy bitterness.

"Looking diligently lest any man fail of the grace of God; lest any root of bitterness springing up trouble you, and thereby many be defiled." Hebrew 12:15 (KJV)

Root of Bitterness Springing Up

"Roots" grow invisibly, below the surface of the soil. The Sunset Western Garden Book states: "At the root ends are tender root tips. Each contains a growing point that continuously produces elongating cells. These cells push the roots deeper and farther out into the moist soil. Roots sap the soil of chemical substances. The first single root soon begins to send out tiopy white rootlets, which draw in the chemical substances needed for growth.

Bitterness can sap up all your energy, leaving you feeling physically, mentally, emotionally, and spiritually bankrupt. Roots give birth to more weeds. If left unchecked, the spreading process will take over and destroy the manicured lawn.

Oftentimes, potential consequences of bitterness can be very damaging. Dewey Bertolini said, "To my surprise and disgust I discovered that my own bitterness was eating me alive. My research revealed that bitterness possesses the potential of destroying you and me in six deadly ways."

First, he looked at physical destruction. When God created mankind, he did not create us to hate. Peter asked Jesus how often he should forgive. Jesus told Peter to forgive his brother "seventy times seven." Matthew 18:22. In other words, forgive every time you are offended. Jesus gave Peter an important principle—important to maintaining good physical health.

Bitterness is like a poison operating in our systems. Dr. S.I. McMillen points out that bitterness can overtime result in "ulcerative colitis, toxic goiters, high blood pressure, and to include heart disease. In addition, there could be other physical disorders such as insomnia, fatigue, or loss of appetite.

The metaphor (dandelion) I used bitterness as you see can be as damaging and way worse, but hope you get the idea how important it is to get rid of or a better word for it is to destroy bitterness. Before it destroys your health, family and friendship or all relationships you have. If bitterness and hate is deep enough, people will hate to see you coming.

By now, you must be saying how do I get rid or destroy bitterness? The love of God covers a multitude of sin. (1 Peter 4:8 KJV/ 1 Peter 4:8 NIV). If you are reading this book now and you are not saved, I suggest you stop reading and give your life to Christ. Ask Him to forgive you and all your sins and come into your heart and save you. You then will have the strength and mindset to let all bitterness and hate go.

Believe it or not, premature aging can set in when we are carriers of bitterness and hate. I had an old friend to share how they knew someone who blamed God for his wife's death and was angry with God for her death. The gentleman was about to get married again and he looked old enough to be the bride's father. However, they were almost the same age.

Mental Destruction

Dr. McMillen writes: "The moment I start hating a man, I become his slave. I can't enjoy my work anymore because he even controls my thoughts. My resentments produce too many stress hormones in my body, and I become fatigued after only a few hours of work. The work I formerly enjoyed is now drudgery. Even vacations cease to give me pleasure. It may be a luxurious car that I drive along a lake fringed with the autumnal beauty of maples, oak, and birch. As far as my experience of pleasure is concerned, I might as well be driving a wagon in mud and rain. The man I hate hounds me wherever I go. I cannot escape his tyrannical grasp on my mind. When the waiter serves me porterhouse steak with French fries, asparagus, crisp salad, and strawberry shortcake smothered with ice cream, it might as well be stale bread and water. My teeth chew the food and I swallow it but the man I hate will not permit me to enjoy it. The man I hate may be many miles from my bedroom, but crueler than any slave driver. He whips my thoughts into such a frenzy that my innerspring mattress becomes a rack of torture. The lowliest of the surfs can sleep, but not I. I really must acknowledge the act that I am a slave to every man on whom I pour the vials of my wrath."

I wonder if you can identify with Dr. McMillen's confession. I cannot say that I have carried bitterness and hatred that deep. But I have certainly had deep hurt and anger and God had to reveal it to me which I shared early on in this book, *The Cleansing Power of Forgiveness*. The man Dr. McMillen wrote about may not have known he felt like he was feeling. If he did, perhaps he did not even care. Perhaps for him every day was like Christmas. Or he was vacationing in the Bahamas for two weeks sipping on martinis. However, he could be a brother in Christ or a sister in Christ and not know an offense is held against them and going on about the father's (God) business. My point here is the offense must be revealed, if not to the person to God with forgiveness. Because you are the one bound in bondage and needs to be set free.

Solomon must have experienced something similar as he lamented, "Better a meal of vegetables where is love than a fattened calf with hatred." Proverbs 15:17 (KJV). I believe Solomon had experienced firsthand the mental anguish that can result when someone's brain becomes so overcome with roots of bitterness and it spreads throughout the mind. I also believe the person may begin to contemplate suicide.

Emotional Destruction

We must not ignore ongoing hatred and bitterness nor the lack of emotional health. I contend bitterness and hatred drain our systems of emotional energy. The results can be very overwhelming and damaging. That is why Paul commanded, "Do not let the sun go down while you are still angry". Ephesians 4:26. Dr. Meier points out "pent up anger is the root of nearly all clinical depression." What the doctor is saying is someone offends you and you are angry from the offense but do not approach the person to solve the situation or the offense.

He (Dr. Meier) went on to say, "one girl described her depression as 'sinking into a bottomless pit and there is nothing I can do to stop it.' She tried desperately to act and feel 'happy', but simply could not get enough emotional energy to be happy. Her friends and even her youth pastor berated her for not displaying the 'Joy of The Lord', branding her a sinner and plunging her even deeper into that bottomless pit.

Bitterness-induced depression can lead to a variety of harmful behavior patterns. Depression feeds on itself as one's thinking becomes progressively more painful people who feel hopeless, helpless, worthless, and guilty become very self-critical and debasing, cyclical in effect, inappropriate thinking. Meier further states, "when adults become depressed, they look and act depressed; when adolescents become depressed, however, they usually act out their depression. In place of a sad affect, an adolescent may appear belligerent, sarcastic, or hostile. Gripped by emotional depression, an otherwise moral teenager may begin to steal, lie, use drugs, or act out sexually."

This person may attempt to take his own life. The "slow but certain suicide" of bitterness may tragically result in a sudden and catastrophic end to the feelings of anger, depression, and hopelessness that bitterness often brings.

<u>Spiritual Destruction</u>

Bertolini states, "Bitterness often dramatically affects a person's relationship with God." Early on, remember I shared how a young lady was angry with God because her baby died. He further states, "We humans are notorious for blaming God for our problems. The thinking often goes something like this: I didn't choose to be born. I certainly didn't choose this family! God is obviously powerful enough to prevent these situations if He wants to. Why did God let this situation happen to me anyway? We find many people asking if God is such a loving God, why didn't He save me from the rape I went through or the molestation my daughter(s) went through?"

I had a conversation with a young woman who is Holy Ghost filled. She said, as tears rolled down her cheeks, "Why did God allow my son to be molested?" I said maybe He did try to show you that the place you were taking him was not a safe place. I really did not have a sound answer for the young mother. I pray that she has forgiven God for the violation of her son and has forgiven herself. I want to be clear, based on the information given to me about the terrible thing that happened to the son. That it was not the mother's fault, nor was it God's fault. I know God is the greater force in the earth, but perhaps at that time the family was not walking with God and it left them without a covering. Therefore, the spirit of perversion was able to act with the idea it had the right to molest the young boy.

Walking in Unforgiveness

When we do not forgive, it opens the door to the enemy (devil) to send in demons to set up in our souls. It can very easily happen when we blame God and everyone around us and not take responsibility for our actions or the action of others because we are not covered by the hand of God. When I say we are not covered, I am saying we do not have a relationship with God. Here we are talking about demons affecting our life. They may manifest in:

Hatred, Bitterness, Arthritis, High Blood Pressure, Ulcers

If you carry unforgiveness so long, it will set up in your soul and you will need deliverance. Demons cannot enter you because God dwells there if you have accepted Jesus as Lord of your life (Been Born Again). However, they can enter your body and soul causing problems. But demons cannot possess you unless you are unsaved (Not Born Again). So many bad things can happen in our lives because of unforgiveness, but great things can and will happen in our lives when we forgive. We must kill the root of bitterness and hatred with love and forgiveness.

Siblings and Bitter Roots

We have looked at how bitter roots can set up in the heart of mankind in many different ways. I want us to look at a biblical family and how jealousy, hatred and bitterness could have destroyed the family. However, we will see God was in control. That family was Jacob, his wives and twelve sons and his daughter, named Minah.

The life of this family starts with Joseph being a model boy. Jacob and his sons lived in Canaan. I reiterate that Joseph was a model boy. He was seventeen years of age. He would go out to feed the animals with his brothers. He would tell his father, Jacob, their evil doings as young men.

Jacob loved Joseph more than his other children. He loved him more because he got him by Rachel whom he really loved in his old age. He made Joseph a coat of many colors. Joseph was hated by his brothers because they saw and knew their father loved him more (favoritism). The favoritism and love Jacob had for Joseph caused hatred to bitterness and thoughts of murder to enter the hearts of Joseph's brothers. They never spoke nicely to Joseph. It got worse when Joseph had two dreams. The first dream Joseph shared with his brothers was how he would rule over them one day. "Behold, we were binding sheaves in the field, and, lo, my sheaf arose, and also stood upright; and behold your sheaves stood round about and made obeisance to my sheaf." Genesis 37:7(KJV) Joseph's brothers hated him all the more. They said to him, "Shalt thou indeed reign over us? Or shalt thou indeed have dominion over us?" Genesis 37:8 (KJV).

The second dream Joseph also shared with his brothers. "The sun and the moon and the eleven stars made obeisance to me." Genesis 37:9 (KJV) Joseph then shared the dream with his father Jacob. Jacob rebuked Joseph and asked him what did that mean? Jacob asked am I and your mother and your brothers supposed to bow down to you?

Envy was added to the brothers' hatred for Joseph. Envy is selfish and unfriendly, grudging of what another enjoys. Verse 9 was "a symbol of Israel (Jacob), the sun representing Jacob, the moon his wives, and the twelve stars, his sons." Joseph's dreams made an impression on Jacob and Joseph's brothers. They incited envy in the brothers, but also deep thought in Jacob who took the dreams as divine indication of events that would affect his family in the future. The dreams also helped prepare Joseph for the suffering he would endure in the future.

The Plot Against Joseph

Joseph's brothers plotted against him. Joseph told his father, Jacob when his brothers were not obeying him when feeding the flock. One day, they saw him coming towards them and talked of killing him. However, his brother, Ruben said to put Joseph in a pit and leave him.

As joseph approached his brothers, they grabbed him and took off his coat of many colors and put him in a pit. They sat down to eat but were full of hatred and strong bitterness. They looked and saw Ishmaelites coming and were headed to Egypt. Judah encouraged his brothers to sell Joseph to the Ishmaelites and they did. The Ishmaelites took Joseph into Egypt. Joseph was sold into Egypt and the brothers had to face Jacob. "And they took Joseph's coat, and killed a kid of the goats and dipped the coat in the blood; And they sent the coat of many colors and they brought it to their father; and said, this have we found know now whether it be thy son's coat or no. And he knew it, and said it and said, it is my son's coat; an evil beast hath devoured him; Joseph is without doubt rent in pieces." Genesis 37:31-33 (KJV) Jacob had been deceived as he deceived his father, Isaac by making him think he was Esau. Deception was an iniquity that flowed through the bloodline.

Joseph Meets His Brothers

A famine had come upon the earth. Jacob saw there was corn in Egypt. He sent all of his sons to get corn except Benjamin. When the sons of Jacob arrived in Egypt, Joseph knew who they were. However, he never let on that he knew them. He tricked them into going back to Canaan to get his brother, Benjamin after he made himself known to his brothers. He wanted them to go and bring his father to Egypt.

> "When he, Joseph, made himself known to his brothers, he had everyone to leave the room. He cried out loud, not caring who heard him. And Joseph said unto his brethren, I am Joseph; doth my father still live? And his brethren could not answer him; for they were troubled at his presence. And Joseph said unto his brethren, come near to me, I pray you. And they came near. And he said, I am Joseph your brother, whom ye sold into Egypt. Now, therefore be not grieved, nor angry with yourselves that ye sold me hither: for God did send me before to preserve life." For these two years hath the famine been in the land: and yet there are five years, in which there shall neither be earing nor harvest. And God sent me before you to preserve your posterity in the earth, and to save your lives by a great deliverance. So now it was not you that sent me hither, but God: And he hath made me a father to Pharoah, and lord of all his house and a ruler throughout all the land of Egypt." Joseph continues to confirm who he is and now Joseph is recognized by his brothers." Genesis 45:3-11 (KJV).

THE CLEANSING POWER OF FORGIVENESS

Now we see how Joseph's heart could have been filled with bitterness and hatred but was not. His brothers' hearts were full of jealousy, envy, hatred, and bitterness. We see they were driven to want to kill him but decided to sell him to the Ishmaelites for twenty pieces of silver and they took Joseph on to Egypt.

When Joseph identified himself to his brothers, he tells them (verses 5-8) do not be angry with yourselves for the evil things you did to me. It was God's will. What the devil meant for evil; God has brought good out of it. He told them that God sent him ahead of them to preserve prosperity for you and save your lives from the famine.

Joseph did not hold a grudge against his brothers. No where do I see he was angry with them. He was blessed through the hurt and pain his brothers put him through. In Egypt, he became the head person; Pharoah put him over everything except his wife who wrongly accused him of sexually attacking her because he refused to sleep with her. God still blessed Joseph and brought him through that. And he was able to bless his whole family during a famine in the land.

What I want us to see is that many things may happen to us, but we must trust God because He can and will bring good out of the situation. "And we know that in all things God works for the good of those who love Him, who have been called according to His purpose." Romans 8:28 (KJV).

Also, if you have the opportunity to help the offender and the Bible says it will be like putting hot coals on top of their heads. The NIV Study Bible says, "You will heap burning coals on his head." Proverbs 25:22a (NIV). Ellicott's Commentary for English Readers says, "thou shalt make him burn with shame at the thought of the wrong he has done thee." The scripture further states, "And the Lord will reward you." God is the rewarder!

CHAPTER SEVEN
UNFORGIVENESS FOR A TOTAL STRANGER

We can have hatred and bitterness for people we do not know. We can and do hate and carry bitterness for people because of the color of their skin; occasionally because of their weight or how they talk. We will say, I cannot stand them. God created all of mankind and said everything He made is good!

We step into the devil's hands by not knowing people. I mean really know them, not just their names, but get to understand them, especially when it comes to race. What is their culture? What are they really about? Ask God to help you to understand them. If you lack salvation, ask God into your heart and His love will help you to understand them.

There are many people who hate and hold bitterness for our former President, Donald Trump. No one really knows him. I only know him by his spirit and, of course, that is who he really is and not the outer form (his flesh). I believe God showed me his heart. He (God) also told me to intercede for him while he was in office. I might add, I am not a Democrat nor Republican, but I am a lover of God the Father and I follow Him by His Spirit.

As previously mentioned in Chapter Five, a young lady who used to be part of a group that I am, passed away. Before she became Ill, because of a message she heard me preach, she made a confession. The theme was "The Cleansing Power of Forgiveness". She stood before the body of Christ and confessed that she held unforgiveness for former President Barack Obama. I had shared in that message how unforgiveness can hide. She stated she did not realize she had unforgiveness in her heart for him until she heard that message. With that message, she forgave him and let it go.

Recovering from Infidelity

Restoration

When we get married, most of us want it to be until death do us apart. However, with some of us it does not happen that way.

I will start with myself. I was sixteen when I got married the first time. There was some infidelity and the marriage lasted seven years. This is my third marriage; however, after salvation and knowing what God tells us about marriage this is a very good and stable marriage. God gives principles for marriage. If we follow those principles, our marriages will last until death do us apart.

I contend forgiveness starts with a decision you must first decide you are going to forgive the person who offended you. Sometimes forgiveness feels impossible, but it is not. Once we think about what Christ did for us, it is not hard nor is it impossible. I am going to use a couple of fictitious examples on forgiveness/unforgiveness. First example: Betty and John were married fresh out of high school. Betty became pregnant shortly after they were married. John's job was working in a factory. Before Betty gave birth to their first child, John started to come home late. Betty did not say anything to John the first few times; however, he became later and later coming home. Finally, Betty said to John, "why are you so late coming home?" John said, "I am just hanging out at the bar with the fellas." Betty became suspicious; however, did nothing about it. Soon she gave birth to a healthy baby boy. A year later, she was pregnant again. John slowed down with staying out late for a while but was back to his old ways.

One evening, Betty decided to go to John's job and follow him after he was off work. John drove straight to his mistress's home. As she met him at the door, they embraced with a kiss. To see that, Betty was deeply hurt. When John returned home, Betty asked for a divorce. John pleaded with Betty to please forgive him, that he would end the affair right then. Betty loved John and she was about to have their second child. Betty forgave John and John also asked God's forgiveness. Because Betty loved God, she was able to forgive her husband, John. However, trust had to be rebuilt by John.

No Restoration

True Story. Many years ago, I met a family, and the father was not in the home. I was told he had moved out to be with his mistress. However, he continued to financially take care of his family. One time, he took his mistress and her children out of town. While they were gone, it snowed and rained on top of the snow. The highway had black ice on it as they traveled back home. The vehicle skidded and overturned. The mistress and her child were killed.

The wife took her husband back and tried to forgive him. She had much bitterness and hurt that she could not forgive him. I might add, she was not a believer. She became a believer later years. But she still held on to the hatred and bitterness she had before salvation. He passed away a few years ago. My prayer is that she will forgive him before she passes away. Remember, God says if we do not forgive, He will not forgive us. I try to live with a forgiving heart. If my husband would get a child by another woman, it would be extremely hard to forgive him and stay with him. I believe forgiveness would not be hard, but I could not stay with him. I really do not know because God has not allowed me to suffer that pain. Praise God.

Restoration vs. Forgiveness

In Galatians 6:1, Paul writes, "Brethren, if a man is overtaken in any trespass, you who are spiritual restore such a spirit of gentleness, considering yourself lest you also be tempted."

Paul is saying to us who are believers to help restore those who are weak. Therefore, we need to know what that means. We need to know that restoration does not equal forgiveness. The two must be separated. Forgiveness can be instantaneous. Restoration is not, especially among people.

When we do not forgive, it places us in bad standing with God. However, when we forgive it places us in good standing with God. And forgiveness should be done immediately. Restoration is a process. Trust has to develop over time. Then you can have forgiveness and restoration.

In our true story, the wife never forgave; therefore, restoration never had a chance before he died.

Remember to forgive and be in right standing with God and restoration will be possible. Restoration and reconciliation are a process based on the attitude and action of the offender. The goal of reconciliation is restoring a broken relationship.

Husband

"Husband loving his wife, just as Christ loved the church and gave himself up for her to make her holy. Cleansing her by the washing with water through the word, and to present her to himself as a radiant church without stain or wrinkle or any other blemish, but holy and blameless. In this same way, husbands ought to love their wives as their own bodies. He who loves his wife loves himself. After all, no one ever hated his own body, but he feeds and cares for it, just as Christ does the church. For we are members of His body. For this reason, a man will leave his father and mother and be united to his wife and the two will become one flesh. This is a profound mystery: but I am talking about Christ and the church. However, each one of you also must love his wife as he loves himself and the wife and the wife must respect her husband. Cornerstone Marriage & Family Ministries".

> "Husbands, love your wives, even as Christ also loved the church, and gave himself for it; That he might sanctify and cleanse it with the washing of water by the word, That he might present it to himself a glorious church, not having spot, or wrinkle or any such thing; but that it should be holy and without blemish." Ephesians 5:25-27 (KJV).

The Husband's Appreciation of Biblical Submission

For a husband, when his wife demonstrates a heart of submission in marriage, she is a pleasure to be around. The husband finds an appreciation and admiration for her because she is one who he can trust. As a result, he can feel at peace and content. He can trust her with his deepest desires and fears because he is not afraid of her scorning him, competing with him or rejecting him. He can relax with her because he knows that even he makes mistakes she will be working with him to help him to put them right. The husband can feel secure in himself that she will be working to minimize the consequences of his mistake rather than trying to prove a point or reject him in some way.

Wife

A man whose wife truly understands, and practices biblical submission acquires a greater sense of self-respect. He knows she respects him as a husband who accepts his responsibility as a leader in the home. He has confidence that she respects him, and she is not in any way trying to belittle him. Biblical submission in marriage is a wife making a choice not to overtly resist her husband's will.

> "Likewise, ye wives, be in subjection to your own husbands; that, if any obey not the word, they also may without the word be won by the conversation of the wives; While they behold your chaste conversation coupled with fear; Whose adorning let it not be that outward adorning of plaiting the hair, and of wearing of gold, or of putting on of apparel; But let it be the hidden man of the heart, in that which is not corruptible, even the ornament of a meek and quiet spirit, which is in the sight of God of great price. For after this manner in the old time the holy women also, who trusted in God, adorned themselves, being in subjection unto their own husbands: Even Sara obeyed Abraham, calling him lord; whose daughters ye are, as long as ye do well, and

are not afraid with amazement. Likewise, ye husbands, dwell with them according to knowledge, giving honour unto the wife as unto the weaker vessel, and a being heirs together of the grace of life, that your prayers be not hindered. Finally, be ye all of one mind, having compassion one of another love as brethren, be pitiful, be courteous: Not rendering evil for evil, or railing for railing; but contrariwise blessing; knowing that ye are there unto-called, that ye should inherit a blessing. For he that will love life, and see good days, let him refrain his tongue from evil, and his lips that they speak no guile: Let hm eschew evil, and do good; let him seek peace and ensue it. For the eyes of the Lord are over the righteous, and his ears are open unto their prayers; but the face of the Lord is against then that do evil. And who is He that will harm you, if ye be followers of that which is good? But and if ye suffer for righteousness' sake, happy are ye: and be not afraid of their terror, neither be troubled; But sanctify the Lord God in your hearts: and be ready always to give an answer to every man that asketh you a reason of the hope that is in you with meekness and fear: Having a good conscience; that, whereas they speak evil of you, as evildoers, they may be ashamed that falsely accuse your good conversation in Christ. For it is better, if the will of God be so, that ye suffer for well-doing, than for evil doing. For Christ also hath once suffered for sins, the just for the unjust, that he might bring us to God, being put to death in the flesh, but quickened by the Spirit: By which also he went and preached unto the spirits in prison, Which sometime were disobedient, when once the longsuffering of God waited in the days of Noah, while the ark was a preparing, wherein few, that is eight souls were saved by water. The like figure whereunto even baptism doth also now save us (not the putting away of the filth of the flesh, but the answer of a good conscience toward God,) by the resurrection of Jesus Christ. Who is gone into heaven, and is on the right hand of God; angels and authorities and powers being made subject unto Him." 1 Peter 3:1-22 (KJV).

"But if they cannot contain, let them marry for it is better to marry than to burn. And unto the married I command, yet not I, but the Lord, Let not the wife depart from her husband." 1 Corinthians 7:9-10 (KJV)

"Wives submit yourselves unto your own husbands, as unto the Lord. For the husband is the head of the wife even as Christ is the head of the church: and he is the saviour of the body." Ephesians 5:22-23 (KJV)

God can restore any and all relationships. It does not make a difference what the offense is. When we receive Jesus as Lord and God comes to live in us, really, we can forgive all hurt and pain.

If we follow God's principles for marriage, we will not find ourselves in an unforgiving place. A place where we have to ask for forgiveness, nor will we need to forgive our spouse.

<u>Forgiving</u>

Each time I forgive, my heart opens. Opening my heart to love, I find the strength to forgive. Holding on to feelings of resentment, grudges or judgement may feel safer. I may want people to change before

I forgive them. But there is another answer: Allowing the in-dwelling of Christ's spirit to open my heart to love. Through the power of Christ in me, I have the strength to release the weight of unforgiveness. Christ's love is stronger than any perceived injury or harm. Another person's unkindness toward me has no power to hurt me. To forgive is to love, and to love is to let the spirit of Christ heal my heart and my life.

"And when ye stand praying, forgive if ye have ought against any: that your Father also which is in heaven may forgive you your trespasses." Mark 11:25 (KJV)

A Prayer For Forgiveness (by Mark Herringshaw)

King David was known as 'a man after God's own heart'. "David loved God, lived with passion and prayed with poetic and transparent honesty. But David was also a sinner. He stole the wife of one of his most loyal soldiers, conceived a child by her and then to cover his deceit murdered the man. But once this crime was exposed by Nathan, the prophet, David turned again to God. His prayer asking for forgiveness is written in the Bible as Psalm 51. Here is a portion of that prayer.

> O loving and kind God, have mercy. Have pity upon me and take away the awful stain of my transgressions. Oh, wash me, cleanse me from this guilt. Let me be pure again. For I admit my shameful deed-it haunts me day and night. It is against you and you alone I sinned and did this terrible thing. You saw it all, and your sentence against me is just. Create in me a new, clean heart, O God, filled with clean thoughts and right desires. Don't toss me aside, banished forever from your presence. Don't take Your Holy Spirit from me. Restore to me

again the joy of your salvation and make me willing to obey you. Amen." Psalm 51:1-12.

All of us need forgiveness. If something is separating you from God, repeat this ancient prayer. Jesus came to make the hope expressed in this prayer a reality for anyone who will ask.

It is significant to FORGIVE!!!

REFERENCES

1. All scriptures quoted are from the King James Version (KJV), except where noted.
2. Cornerstone Marriage & Family Ministries, 6/30/2021, pages 1-7, www.marriageministry.org/thebiblical-meaning-of-submission-in-marriage-for-wives/
3. Jordan Zakarin (update: March 16, 2021/original July 16, 2020), www.biography.com/news/Menendez-brothers-murder-case-facts
4. Mark Herringshaw, "A Prayer for Forgiveness" Article posted by https://blog.beliefnet.com/prayerplainandsimple/2009/07/a-prayer-for-forgiveness.html#ixzzYaQ753FF
5. Dr. Ned Hallowell, "Dare to Forgive", Four Steps to Forgiveness, Article
6. Robert Karen, Ph.D., "Forgiving Our Parents, Resolving Resentment, Developing Realistic Expectations". Article (page 1). From the May 2003 issue of O, The Oprah Magazine, https://www.oprah.com/article/omagazine/omag200305parents
7. Joyce Meyer, "Six Ways to Find Unforgiveness and Remove It" Article, https://study.joycemeyer.org/
8. Merriam Webster, Webster's New Collegiate Dictionary Definitions of *Forgiveness* (Page 447) and *Unforgiveness* (Page 1269) Copyright 1981.

9. Barry G. Johnson, Sr., "Unforgiveness Characteristics", www.barryjohnsonsr.com. Article Pages 1-6.
10. Grace Valley Christian Center, by P.G. Matthew, M.A., M.Div., Th. M., "Forgiving and Forgiveness" Article, Pages 1-8.
11. Grace Valley Christian Center, by P.G. Matthew, M.A., M.Div., Th. M., "Forgiving and Forgiveness" Article.
12. Robert D. Jones, Assistant Professor of Biblical Counseling at Southeastern Baptist Theological Seminary, Wake Forest NC., *"Forgiveness–I Just Can't Forgive Myself"*, Resources for Changing Lives Book, P&R Publishing, 2000.
13. Dewey Bertolini, *"Secret Wounds and Silent Cries"*, Subtitle: *"Winning Your Personal Battle with Bitterness"* Book, 1993, Pages 30-34.

ABOUT THE AUTHOR

Loreatha Gunnels-Mayberry was born in Morrilton, Conway County, Arkansas. She is one of ten children of Matthew and Minnie Blackmon Gunnels, natives of South Carolina. Mr. Gunnels was a sharecropper, sawmill laborer, and railroad worker.

In her teens she moved to Kansas City, Missouri and then later to Omaha, Nebraska, where she worked and attended school. She graduated from the University of Nebraska at Omaha in 1979 with a degree in criminal justice. While working on her master's degree in 1991, she received a higher calling. Loreatha answered the call of the Holy Spirit and became an ordained minister in 1996.

Loreatha is founder and executive director of Setting the Captives Free, an organization that is designed to rescue, restore, and release women and their children back into the community. God gave her grace in deliverance, healing the deaf, and healing of joints and bones.

God gave Loreatha the name Bethesda Worship and Deliverance Center. On November 1, 2008, Loreatha and her wonderful husband, Melvin Mayberry, who assists her in both endeavors, planted a church in Omaha, Nebraska, using the name that God had revealed to her.

The mother of five adult children, she currently ministers to the women at the Women's Correctional Center in York, Nebraska, in addition to speaking at various churches. She is also a part of other community organizations including North Omaha Village.

**In 2007, Loreatha published her first book, a biographical sketch of her life from childhood through adulthood—*Beyond the Tears: From Misery to Joy*. She published her second book, *Holy Spirit, The Deliverer*, to assist individuals of all ages in their quest for spiritual freedom by showing them how lives can be changed positively through ministering the way to receive deliverance and remain free of the demons that plague our lives. It is her hope that this book, *The Cleansing Power of Forgiveness,* will give the understanding that unforgiveness can and will hide.

LOREATHA GUNNELS MAYBERRY (Biography)

Loreatha Gunnels Mayberry was born January 12, 1943, Morrilton, Conway County, Arkansas (Morrilton is about 48 miles west of the capital city of Little Rock, Arkansas). She was one of ten children of

Matthew and Minnie Blackmon Gunnels, natives of South Carolina. Mr. Gunnels was a sharecropper, sawmill laborer and railroad worker. Mr. Gunnels passed away in 1949 before Loreatha started to school.

Loreatha attended Sarah Clark Elementary School and L.W. Sullivan High School in Morrilton, Arkansas through 8th grade. She, Loreatha, married at age 16. She and her husband became parents of Gary Lynn before they moved to Kansas City in 1961. She moved to Omaha, Nebraska in July, 1961 where she worked at Tip Top Products factory for twelve years while raising a family of five children. Loreatha became the mother of four additional children: Vickie, Artez, Reginald and Kimberly Young.

After she was laid off from Tip Top Products, she returned to school to finish her high school education and gained the impetus to go further. She enrolled at the University of Nebraska at Omaha in 1976. She attended year-round and graduated early in December 1979 with a degree in Criminal Justice.

During the time Loreatha was attending college she suffered major losses. Her mother died on December 5, 1976. The school made arrangements for her to make up exams that she would miss while she was at home with her family.

She completed 12 hours toward a master's degree in Public Administration while she was employed in Security at the University. Three security jobs followed the UNO employment: Douglas County Correction Center, Omaha Correctional Center East Omaha Facility and Omaha Public Power District.

Loreatha received a higher calling. She answered the call of the Holy Spirit in 1991 and was ordained as an Evangelist in 1996. 1996 was an incredible year for Loreatha. In February of that year, she heard from The Lord that she would later be 'called' to Pastor a church. She specifically remembers that encounter being at 5:30 p.m. because it was an audible voice from God.

Loreatha founded an organization in 1999 called, **"Setting the Captives Free."** The purposes of Setting the Captives Free are to provide services to men and women while they are incarcerated and to provide services to men and women after they are released from incarceration. Such services shall include assisting them in obtaining adequate housing, teaching them parenting skills; teaching them life skills; and helping them to secure gainful employment. She serves as Chief Executive Officer of STCF.

Also in 1999, Loreatha became an Apostle of Jesus Christ 'called' by God.

Loreatha is assisted in her endeavors by her current spouse, Melvin Mayberry, who assists in her pastoral duties and with Setting the Captives Free. She is a member of North Omaha Village Organization and works with other community organizations.

After her preparation to move into the calling, Loreatha was given a name by God: Bethesda Worship and Deliverance Center. On November 1, 2008, Loreatha and her husband, Melvin Mayberry, planted a church in Omaha, using the name that God gave her. Bethesda met in the basement of their home for one year and later rented space at World Fellowship Christian Center. As the church grew, they moved to their own space at 7012 Maple Street where they currently serve. Most recently the church held its first Women's Retreat and Annual Prayer Breakfast.

Loreatha authored her first book, *"Beyond the Tears"* in 2007. Her second book, *"Holy Spirit, the Deliverer"* was published in 2014 and the goal of this book is to be published in 2021 as she continues to grow her church.

CONTACT THE AUTHOR

The author may be contacted by email:

stcfree@cox.net

Made in the USA
Columbia, SC
28 April 2022

59600096R00055